TOILET HUMOUR NUMBER 2's

A second selection of bad taste cartoons
from the Silvey–Jex Partnership

FIRST PRINTED IN ENGLAND BY MERLIN COLOUR PRINTERS, CANVEY ISLAND.
ISBN 0 907280 07 2

MOBILE
LOO

"Another one of those 'super-glue' victims Doctor."

Please
replace lid
after use

AAASHOO..!!

SAFARI PARK
LAVATORY

FRARP

"Bloody High-Speed trains!"

PERFUMES
TOILET WATERS

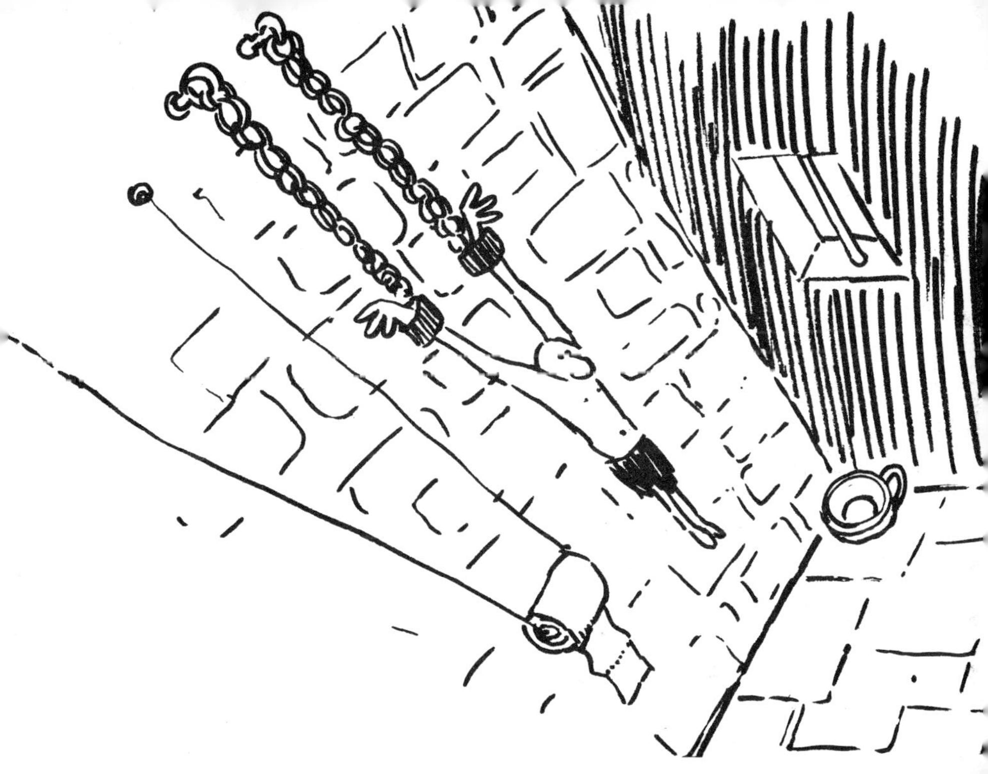

"Oops... sorry dear."

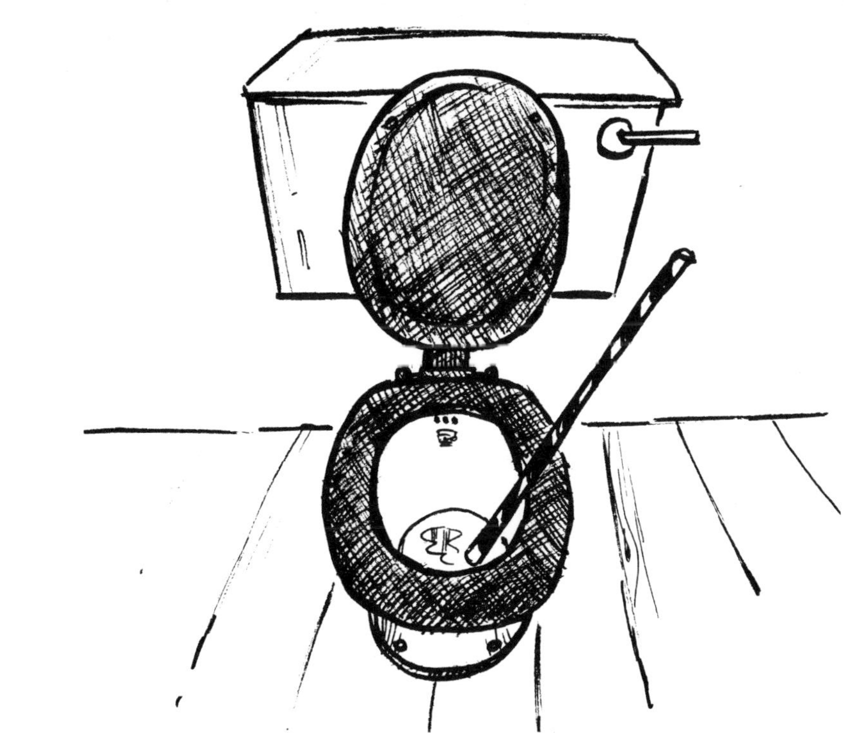

"Hold on I'm coming!"

ROLLER
ROLL
LIMITED

"Why can't you just rinse your mouth out like any other boxer?"

THE GREAT
HENRI.
ILLUSIONIST

"We like to test every loo personally before we leave Madam"

"Bloody loo's blocked again."